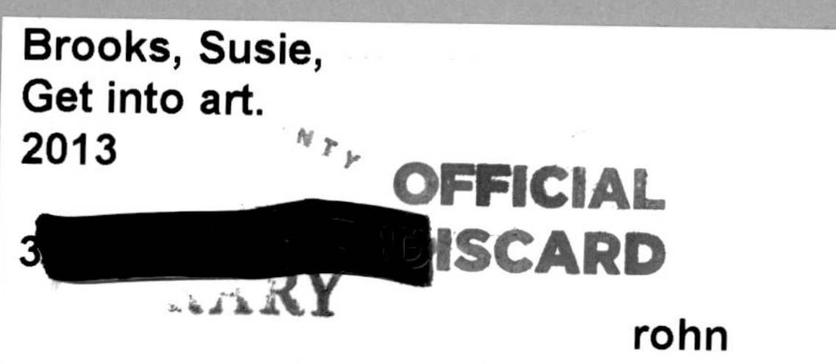
Brooks, Susie,
Get into art.
2013
OFFICIAL
DISCARD
rohn

W9-BNU-708

GET INTO ART

ANIMALS

SUSIE BROOKS

KINGFISHER
NEW YORK

LONDON & NEW YORK

Published in the United States by Kingfisher,
175 Fifth Ave., New York, NY 10010
Kingfisher is an imprint of Macmillan Children's Books, London.

Distributed in the U.S. and Canada by Macmillan,
175 Fifth Ave., New York, NY 10010

Edited by Catherine Brereton
Designed by Jane Tassie
Project photography by Geoff Dann

Library of Congress Cataloging-in-Publication data has been applied for.

ISBN: 978-0-7534-7058-9

Kingfisher books are available for special promotions and premiums. For details contact:
Special Markets Department, Macmillan, 175 Fifth Ave., New York, NY 10010.

For more information, please visit www.kingfisherbooks.com

Printed in China
9 8 7 6 5 4 3 2
2TR/1013/LFG/UG/140MA

Picture credits

The Publisher would like to thank the following for permission to reproduce their material. Every care has been taken to trace copyright holders. However, if there have been unintentional omissions or failure to trace copyright holders, we apologize and will, if informed, endeavor to make corrections in any future edition.
Top = t; Bottom = b; Center = c; Left = l; Right = r
Cover and page 26 *Portrait of Maurice* by Andy Warhol/The National Galleries of Scotland, Edinburgh; page 6 *The Snail* by Henri Matisse/The Tate Gallery, London; 8 *Suspense* by Edwin Landseer/V & A Museum, London/Bridgeman Art Gallery; 10 *Crinkly Giraffe* by Alexander Calder/The Calder Foundation/Private Collection/Bridgeman Art Library; 12 *The Bird* by Georges Braque/Private Collection/Bridgeman Art Library; 14 *Peacock and Magpie* by Edward Bawden/with the kind permission of Peyton Skipwith/Fry Art Gallery, Saffron Walden/ Bridgeman Art Gallery; 16 *Fish (E59)* by M. C. Escher/The Escher Foundation, The Netherlands; 18 *Carnival of Harlequin* by Joan Miró/Albright-Knox Art Gallery, Buffalo/The Art Archive; 20 Shutterstock/Terry Alexander; 21 Shutterstock/2009fotofriends; 22 *Yellow Cow* by Franz Marc/ Solomon R. Guggenheim Museum, New York City/AKG London; 24 Bridgeman Art Library/ Paul Freeman; 28 *Jockeys in the Rain* by Edgar Degas/CSG CIC Glasgow Museums Collection.

CONTENTS

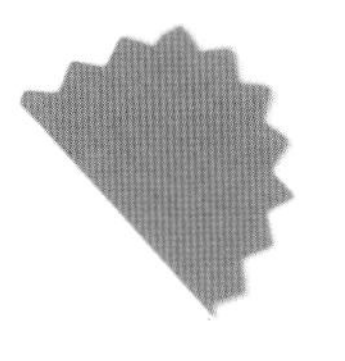

PICTURE AN ANIMAL

If you were going to draw an animal, what would it be? You have so much choice, it might be hard to decide! Animals are a great subject for artists because there are so many shapes, colors, and characters to choose from. Friendly pets, fierce wild beasts, bright birds, and even imaginary creatures have made their way into paintings, sculptures, and other works of art.

Look at the different ways in which **animals have inspired famous artists**—and then **let them inspire you, too!** Each page of this book will tell you about a work of art and the person who created it. When you lift the flap, you'll find a project based on the artwork. Don't feel you have to copy it exactly. Half the fun of art is making something your own!

GETTING STARTED

There's a checklist on page 31 that will tell you what you need for each project, but it's a good idea to read through the steps before you begin. There are also some handy tips on the next page . . .

Always have a **pencil** and **eraser** handy. Making a rough **sketch** can help you plan a project and see how it's going to look.

PICK YOUR PAINT . . .

Acrylic paints are thick and bright—they're great for strong colors and for textures such as shaggy fur. **Poster paints** are cheaper than acrylics but still bright. Use them when you need a lot of paint.

Watercolors give a thinner coloring—try them over oil pastel or crayon, or draw over them in ink.

Use a mixture of thick and thin **paintbrushes**. Have a glass jar or plastic cup of water ready to rinse them in and a **palette** or paper plate for mixing paint.

acrylic paint

Lay some newspaper on your surface before you start to paint!

watercolor paint

sponged paint

TRY PASTELS . . .

Oil pastels have a bright, waxy look, like crayons. **Soft pastels** can be smudged and blended like chalk.

oil pastels

soft pastel

For painting, use thick **drawing** or **watercolor paper**—anything too thin will wrinkle. **Pastel paper** has a rough surface that holds on to the color.

Collect a range of **colored paper and card stock** for collages and 3-D models.

Look around the home for other art materials. Useful things include sponges, rags or cloths, toothpicks, drinking straws, scissors, glue, string, roller brushes, and a hole punch.

Ready to start?
Let's **get into art!**

In real life, this picture is enormous —almost 10 feet (3 meters) square! It's a collage of painted paper stuck onto white paper and then onto canvas. Matisse called this method "drawing with scissors."

THE SNAIL

Henri Matisse 1953

You might have to look twice before spotting the snail in this picture! There's no outline, but Henri Matisse has created the idea of a snail by arranging colored shapes in a spiral pattern.

Drawing with color

When Matisse made *The Snail*, he was 84 years old. He wasn't well enough to stand and draw, so instead he used color as his starting point. His assistants painted sheets of paper in plain colors, and then Matisse cut or tore them into shapes.

Matisse chose his colors carefully. They are not the colors of a real snail, but they are warm and bright. Matisse knew that complementary colors, such as red and green, look stronger when they're put next to each other. The way he has placed the pieces makes them zing out, as if the snail is moving. It seems to be wriggling out of the jagged orange frame!

WHO WAS MATISSE?

Henri Matisse was born in France in 1869. His first job was as a lawyer, but he didn't like it much. At the age of 20, he became ill and had to spend long hours in bed. His mother gave him a paint box to pass the time, and right away he knew he would become an artist! Matisse made many famous paintings in his distinctive, colorful style.

SUSPENSE

Sir Edwin Landseer 1861

Who is this dog waiting for? What's behind the door? Landseer wanted us to ask questions like this when he painted *Suspense*! His picture tells a story, but he leaves us to figure out what it is.

See the story

If you look closely, you'll spot some clues. There are drops of blood on the floor . . . a feather torn from a hat . . . a knight's armored gloves on the table. It seems that the dog's master has been wounded and carried through the house.

The dog sits on his haunches, staring closely at the door. We can tell that he is worried and longs to rush to his master's side. Landseer's skillful brushwork makes us feel that the animal is alive. The light glints on his anxious face, and hairs stand up on his neck. He leans forward, ready to spring up at any moment—but we can only imagine what he'll find.

WHO WAS LANDSEER?

Sir Edwin Landseer was born into a family of artists in England in 1802. He began to draw as soon as he could hold a pencil and was exhibiting work by the age of 13. Animals were his favorite subjects—he even had a breed of dog named after him! Landseer made sculptures, too, including four huge bronze lions in London's Trafalgar Square.

CRINKLY GIRAFFE

Alexander Calder 1971

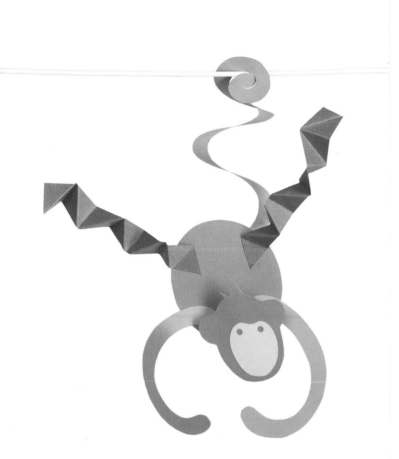

This giraffe isn't going anywhere—but if you walk around it, it almost seems to move. Calder was famous for his dynamic sculptures, some of which really do move.

Animobiles

Crinkly Giraffe is made of painted metal cut into simple shapes. The flat metal looks different from different angles, so the crinkly neck seems to shift and turn. Calder made a whole series of crinkly animals like this. His wife named them animobiles!

The word *animobile* comes from *animal* and *mobile*—and Calder invented the mobile, too. His first one had a motor, but he soon realized that hanging shapes would move on their own. He experimented with different materials, including metal, wire, and wood. Little did he know how popular his invention would become!

In 1926, Calder made a whole circus of animals and actors out of wood, wire, cork, and cloth. He kept them in suitcases and traveled around giving performances!

WHO WAS CALDER?

Alexander Calder was born in 1898 in the United States. His father was a sculptor and his mother a painter, but Alexander studied to be an engineer. Later, he went to art school and traveled to Paris, France, to work. He used nature as his inspiration for abstract mobiles, standing "stabiles," and giant outdoor sculptures that are displayed around the world.

G.B

THE BIRD

Georges Braque 1949

On first glance, you might think a child made this picture! The shapes are simple and the colors are bright. In fact, Braque created it for children, as part of a project for schools in the United Kingdom after World War II.

Primary print

The idea came from a woman in London, England who decided that schools should have great pieces of art on their walls. She traveled to Paris, France, and persuaded artists such as Braque to help. They produced work using a new type of lithograph printing. Each print had a border around the edge, so there wasn't any need for a frame!

Braque was fond of bold, simple shapes—and he particularly loved painting birds. In this print, the shapes are familiar, but they float in an imaginary scene. The primary colors red, yellow, and blue look cheerful and fresh against the white.

WHO WAS BRAQUE?

Georges Braque was born in France in 1882. He trained as a painter and decorator but studied art in the evenings and soon took up Fauvism—a new style of painting in bright colors. He then turned to Cubism, using simple shapes and collage. During World War I, he was injured and had to stop painting. Later, he experimented with prints and sculpture.

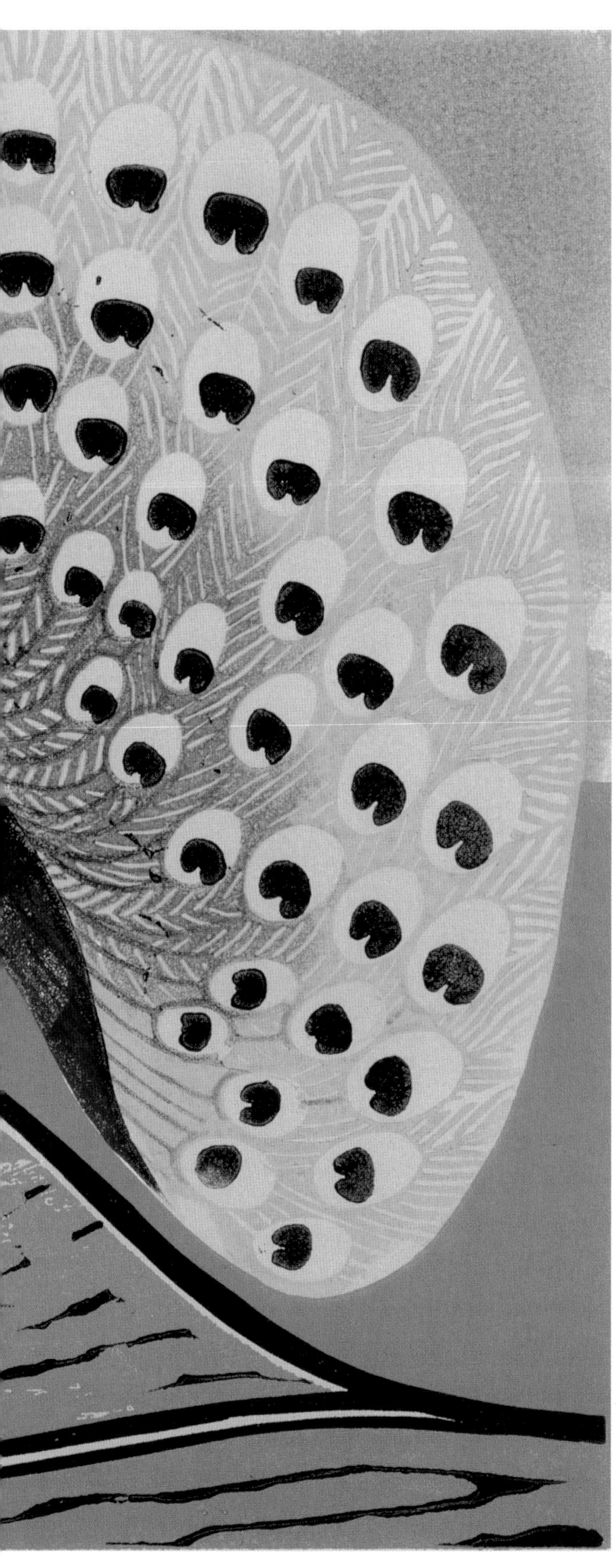

PEACOCK AND MAGPIE

Edward Bawden 1970

What's the first thing you notice in this picture? Probably the peacock with its dazzling, fanned-out tail! Bawden shows us the proud character of the bird in this illustration of one of Aesop's Fables.

A telling tail

Fables are stories with a moral, which means they have a lesson to teach us. In this one, the peacock declares that he should be king of the birds. The others are impressed by his grand appearance, but the magpie questions whether he could protect the birds against eagles and other hunters. The moral is to listen to the advice of others.

Bawden cut this scene into linoleum and then printed it in ink on paper. The crisp lines make the story clear, but they are decorative, too. The yellow of the peacock catches our eye, just as it attracts the birds. Only when we look more closely do we see the magpie talking wisely to the crowd.

WHO WAS BAWDEN?

Edward Bawden was born in England in 1903. He became famous for many types of art, including book illustrations, advertising posters, murals, and metalwork furniture. He made tile paintings for the London Underground (the subway) and even designed china for passenger ships!

FISH (E59)

M. C. Escher 1942

No matter how hard you look, you won't find a gap between these fish! Escher has taken the shape of an animal and turned it into a perfect pattern. It's called a tessellation.

Tile style

Tessellation is basically tiling—every shape fits together edge to edge. Of course, it's much harder to tile an animal shape than a simple square or triangle! Escher used geometric shapes as his starting point, then changed them into curving forms. He twisted, flipped, and repeated them to make patterns.

We can see two types of fish in this picture. It's like looking through a kaleidoscope. Escher drew them on graph paper and then colored them with pencils, ink, and watercolor. He liked the idea that the pattern could go on forever, though he had to stop when he got near the edge of the page!

Escher made 137 drawings like this one. He created patterns using lizards, frogs, insects, birds, and even human shapes. His work has always fascinated mathematicians—but surprisingly, Escher struggled with math in school!

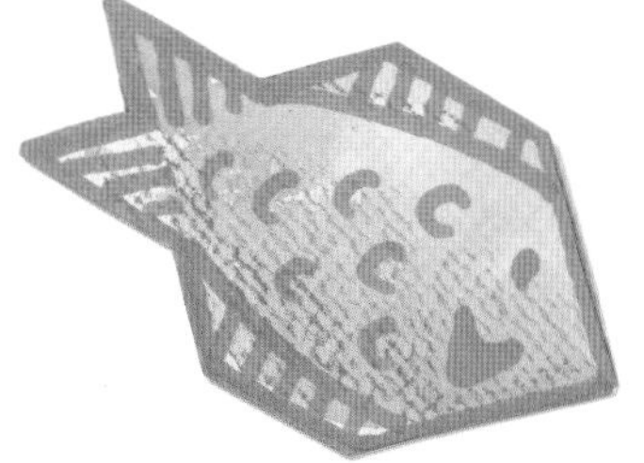

WHO WAS ESCHER?

Maurits Cornelis Escher was born in the Netherlands in 1898. His interest in linking shapes began on a trip to the Alhambra, a Moorish castle in Spain. He drew and sketched on his travels and went home to make prints of the buildings he'd seen. In his work, he loved to trick the eye and play with impossible spaces. He turned the world into a puzzling and unbelievable place!

CARNIVAL OF HARLEQUIN

Joan Miró 1924–1925

Have you ever seen things in a dream that wouldn't make sense in real life? Miró takes us to a dreamlike place in this painting of a strange but lively party!

Carnival chaos

The creatures here aren't animals as we know them, but you can probably recognize some shapes. There are winged insects, spidery forms, a fish, and two cats playing with string. Bright characters leap across the canvas, dancing to musical notes that are floating in the air.

When Miró painted this, he was poor and hungry. Perhaps that's why the main figure, the Harlequin, has a hole in his guitar-shaped stomach. He looks sad and still in this happy, playful scene. Miró said that hunger made him hallucinate, or see things that weren't really there.

WHO WAS MIRÓ?

Joan Miró was born in Spain in 1893. On a trip to Paris, France, in the 1920s, he became interested in an art style called Surrealism. He was fascinated by people's imaginations, especially children's, and became famous for his colorful paintings and sculptures that seem to come from a make-believe world.

The Thunderbird brings thunder with his flapping wings and lightning with a flash of his eyes! Below him is Sea-Bear and a killer whale, then a man with a frog. Lower down we see the yellow-nosed Bakwas—"wild man of the woods"—and Dzunukwa, a child-eating giantess. They are all characters from Kwakwaka'wakw legend.

TOTEM POLES

Wayne Alfred and Beau Dick 1991 and Ellen Neel 1955 (near left)

It's hard to imagine that these colorful carvings began life as whole cedar trees! Totem poles show the skill of traditional artists from the northwest coast of North America.

Tall stories

It can take a year to carve a totem pole! The idea is to tell a story, perhaps about an event, a legend, or people in a particular family. Each pole is a stack of characters that have special meaning in the local culture. Many animals and birds are believed to have special powers or to bring different kinds of luck.

The green-faced figure on the far left is Red Cedar Bark Man. In traditional tales, he survived a great flood and gave people the first canoe. You can see him holding a patterned boat, with the legendary Quolus bird spreading its wings above him. Quolus is the younger brother of Thunderbird, who tops the pole on the near left.

TOTEM TRADITION

Native Americans have carved totem poles for hundreds of years, but because wood rots, the oldest examples have not survived. These two were made by modern-day artists from the Kwakwaka'wakw tribe of British Columbia, Canada. You can tell they are modern because of the bright paint colors.

YELLOW COW

Franz Marc 1911

Have you ever seen a yellow cow with blue spots? Probably not! Franz Marc loved to paint from nature, but he didn't copy exactly what he saw.

Inside out

Marc said that he wanted to re-create animals "from the inside." He used colors to express different feelings. For him, yellow was cheerful, gentle, and female—like this cow, leaping happily across a sunny scene.

Marc's style of painting is known as Expressionism. It captures a mood rather than a realistic view of the world and makes us look at things in a different way. In fact, Marc knew very well how to paint a realistic cow. He spent long hours sketching and studying animals and even taught other artists about their shape and form.

WHO WAS MARC?

Franz Marc was born in Germany in 1880, the son of a landscape painter. He took up art at the age of 20 and was soon organizing exhibitions with other Expressionist artists. Marc was fascinated by animals. He wanted to paint the world through their eyes. Sadly, he died young, fighting in World War I.

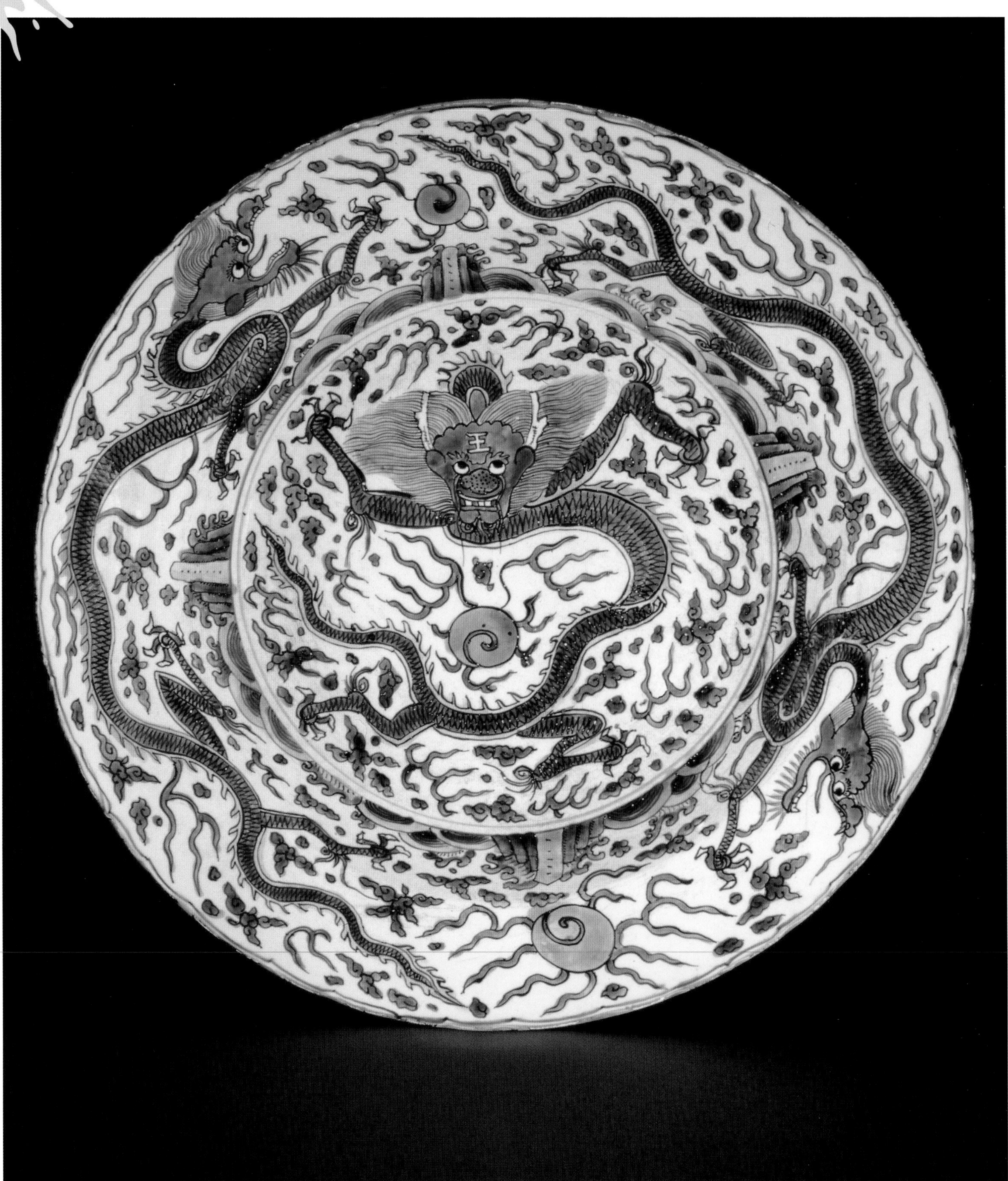

DRAGON DISH

Chinese artist 1600–1635

When this dish was made, artists didn't have paints like ours. Instead they used pigments—solid cakes of color that they ground into powder and mixed with liquid. This blue comes from a substance called cobalt. It has been used in Chinese pottery for more than 1,000 years.

A snake's body, an eagle's claws, the scales of a fish . . . you can see several animals in a Chinese dragon!
These dragons are painted on a porcelain dish, surrounded by decorative swirls.

Curious creatures

Artists can have fun with dragons because they're imaginary—no one really knows what they look like! In Chinese mythology, they are often friendly, unlike the fire-breathing dragons of Europe. They are rulers of water and the weather and symbols of power and good luck.

These three dragons have lizardlike head frills and wriggling bodies that twist around the dish. Their four claws show that they are ordinary dragons—five claws would mean they belonged to an emperor. The round shapes that the dragons are chasing are magical flaming pearls. Everything is painted in a single color—cobalt blue. The artist used a fine brush for the detail and then filled in the outlines. In some parts, the color is layered to give a darker effect.

HOW WAS IT MADE?

This type of ceramic painting is called "underglaze blue." The blue design is painted onto dried white porcelain and then coated with a clear protective glaze. Afterward it is baked, or fired, at a high temperature. This hardens the porcelain and sets the glaze.

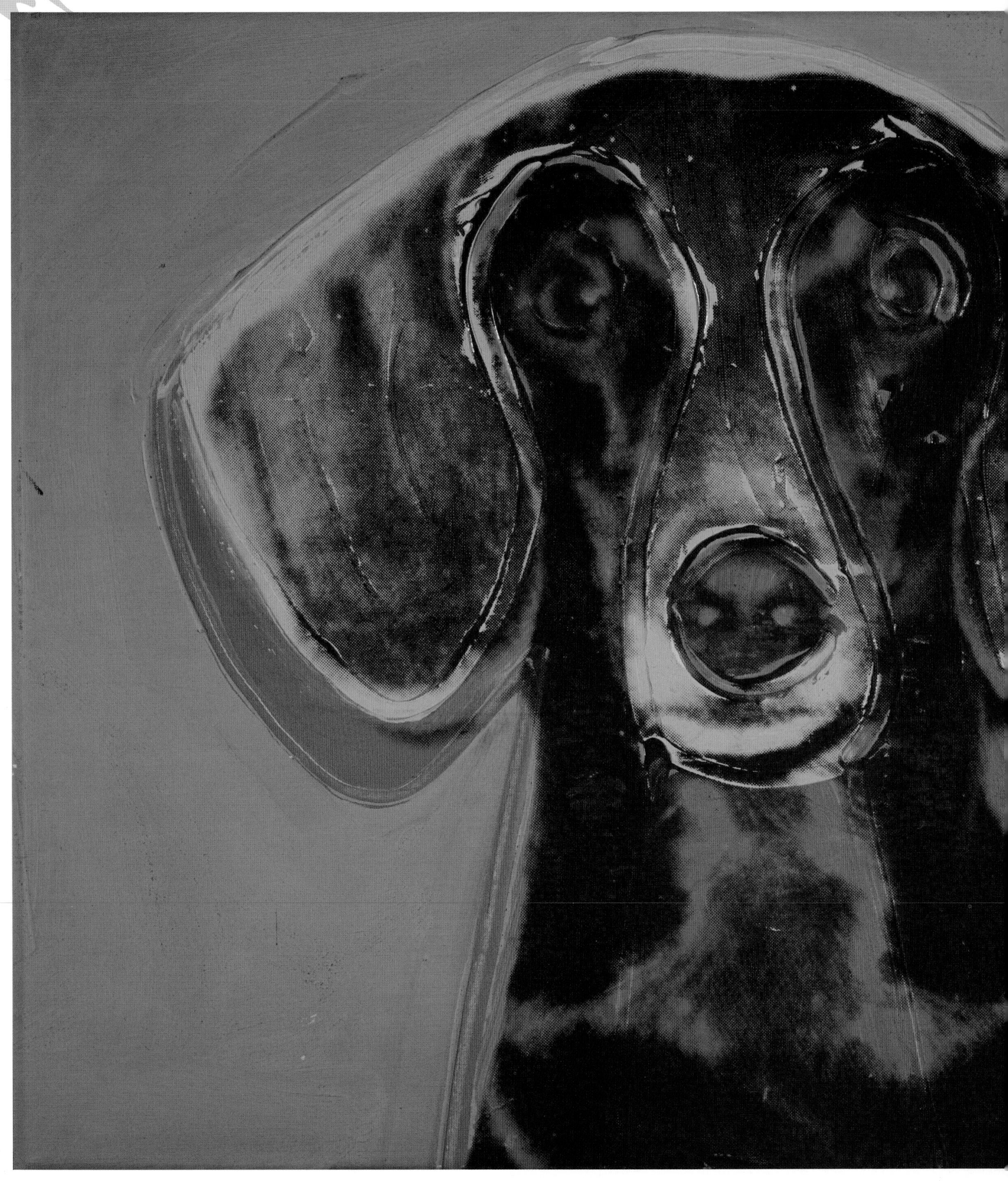

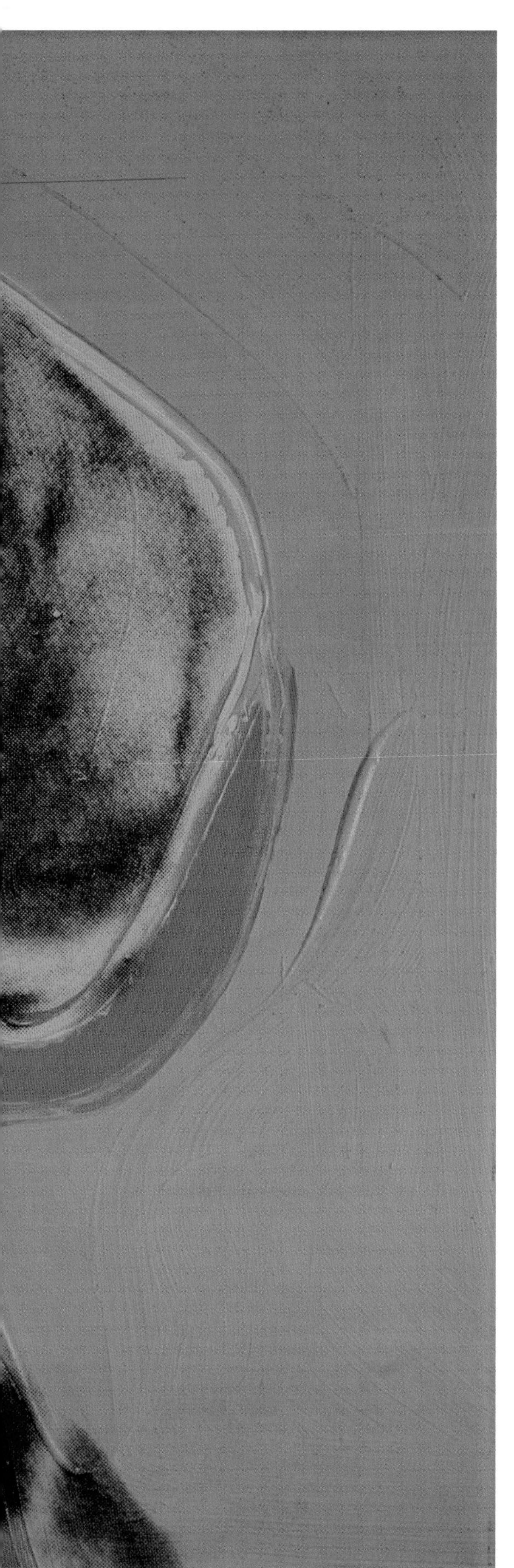

PORTRAIT OF MAURICE

Andy Warhol 1976

Andy Warhol was known for his pictures of rich and famous people—but he happily made portraits of their pets, too! This dachshund belonged to the art collector Gabrielle Keiller.

Dazzling dog

Maurice the dachshund wasn't actually blue, pink, and red! Warhol liked experimenting with bold, attention-grabbing colors—they reminded him of advertisements and modern life. He took photographs of Maurice and then worked on them back in his studio. To make this screen print, he pushed ink through a type of stencil on a silk screen.

Warhol once wrote, "I never met a pet I didn't like"—and, in fact, he had two dachshunds of his own. You can see his love of animals in this portrait of Maurice, who looks straight at us with appealing eyes.

WHO WAS WARHOL?

Andy Warhol was born in the United States in 1928. His talent for art showed from a young age, and he loved movies, photography, and cartoons. He became famous for his Pop Art inspired by advertising images and glamorous stars. Archie, one of his dachshunds, was often photographed by his side!

Degas

JOCKEYS IN THE RAIN

Edgar Degas *about* 1883–1886

Looking at this picture, we know just how the horses are feeling! Degas shows us their nerves and excitement before a race, with the added restlessness of a storm.

Stormy start

Strong, colorful marks bring this pastel scene to life. Degas has drawn long streaks of blue to show the thrashing fall of rain. His diagonal strokes of green make the grass seem to sway, and the distant trees lean in the wind.

Notice how the horses are kept to one side of the drawing—some are even cut off at the picture's edge. Degas wanted us to feel the tension as the horses wait in a line. Their poses are full of movement, as if they're ready to charge ahead over the open ground.

WHO WAS DEGAS?

Edgar Degas was born in France in 1834. By the age of 18, he had created his own art studio. He loved to make pictures of everyday scenes and was fascinated by dancers and horses and how they moved. The way he cropped his figures and showed them from odd angles was seen as very daring at the time.

ART WORDS AND INFO

abstract Not representing an actual object, place, or living thing. Abstract art often focuses on simplified shapes, lines, colors, or use of space.

carving An artwork made by cutting into a solid material, such as wood or stone.

collage A picture made by sticking pieces of paper, fabric, or other objects onto a surface.

complementary colors Colors that are opposite each other on the color wheel (see panel below). If you place complementary colors next to each other, they look brighter.

Cubism (1907–1920s) An art style that involved making images using simple geometric shapes.

exhibit To display work for people to see—for example, in a gallery or museum.

Expressionist From the art style Expressionism (1905–1920s). Expressionist art was about feelings and emotions, often shown through distorted shapes or colors.

Fauvism (about 1905–1910) An art style that focused on strong, vibrant colors and bold brushstrokes.

illustration A picture that explains or decorates a story or other text.

linoleum A tough, washable material with a smooth surface. Artists can scrape a design into it and then cover it with paint or ink to make a print.

lithograph A type of print in which the design is drawn onto stone or metal with a greasy substance. This is then covered with ink, which clings only to the greasy areas, and printed onto paper.

mural A picture painted directly onto a wall.

COLOR CONNECTIONS

In art there are three primary colors—**red**, **yellow**, and **blue**. These are colors that can't be mixed from any others. Each primary color has has an opposite, or complementary, color, which is made by mixing the other two.

If you mix a color with its complementary color, you'll get a shade of brown.

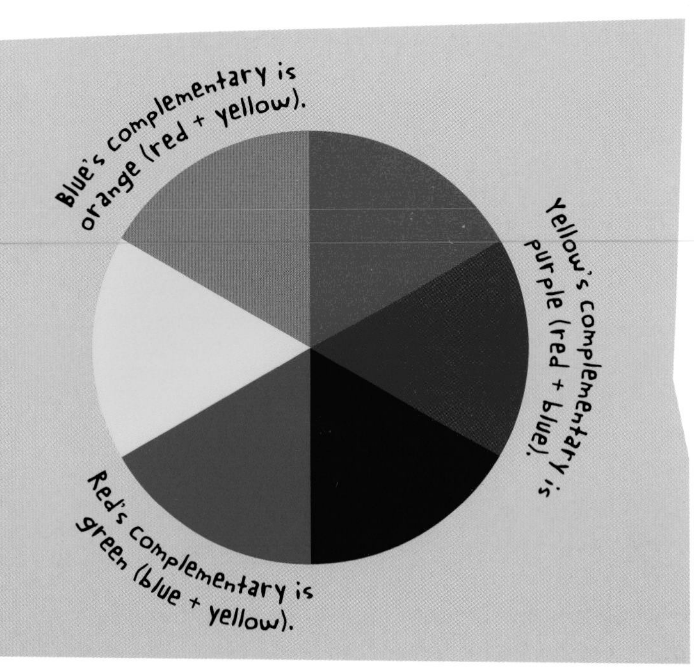

Blue's complementary is orange (red + yellow).
Yellow's complementary is purple (red + blue).
Red's complementary is green (blue + yellow).

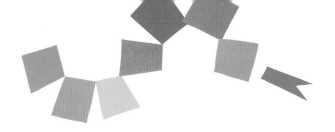

Pop Art (mid-1950s–1960s) An art style that celebrated the bold, bright images of advertising, cartoon strips, and modern life.

porcelain A white, clay-based material that is used to make china (or ceramics).

print A way of transferring an image from one surface to another. Prints are often made by spreading ink over a raised or engraved design and then pressing it onto paper. This makes a reverse or negative image that can be reproduced many times.

screen print A print made by dragging ink over a stencil marked onto a silk screen. The ink goes through tiny holes in the silk that aren't covered by the stencil.

sculpt To make three-dimensional art, called sculpture. Carving and clay modeling are both types of sculpture. Someone who does this is called a sculptor.

sketch A rough drawing or painting, often made to help plan a final artwork.

stencil A template that allows paint or ink to go through the holes but blocks out other areas.

studio A place where an artist or photographer works.

Surrealism (1924–1940s) An art style that explored the world of dreams, the imagination, and the "nonthinking" mind. Surrealist works often show familiar things but in unexpected or impossible ways.

symmetrical When one side of a shape is the mirror image of the other side.

texture The feel of a surface, such as rough fur or smooth scales.

PROJECT CHECKLIST

These are the materials you'll need for each project. The ones in parentheses are useful, but you can manage without them!

Snip a snake (page 7): white card stock or posterboard, brightly colored papers, scissors, glue

Furry friends (page 9): acrylic paints, paintbrushes, sponge, toothpick

Crinkly monkeys (page 11): colored card stock, scissors, hole punch, glue

Seaside string print (page 13): stiff cardboard, pencil, craft glue, thick string or cord, scissors, sponge or roller, thick paint, white paper, colored paper, (bubble wrap, sponge cloth, drinking straws)

Fabulous feathers (page 15): thick white paper or card stock, pencil, oil pastels, acrylic paints, paintbrushes, (toothpick, teaspoon)

Fish squish (page 17): graph paper, thin card stock, glue, ruler, pencil, scissors, tape, white paper, coloring materials (for example, markers, oil pastels, watercolor paint, paintbrushes)

Crazy creatures (page 19): thick white paper, black crayon, water-based paints, paintbrushes, (modeling clay)

Crafty totem (page 21): cardboard tube, different colored papers, ruler, tape, pencil or chalk, scissors, (zigzag scissors), glue, stiff card stock

Moody sheep (page 23): thick white paper, glue, sponge, bright paints, palette or paper plate, large piece of paper or posterboard, paintbrush, scissors

Dishy dragon (page 25): paper plate, pencil, blue paint, fine paintbrush, wide paintbrush, (glitter or glitter paint)

Colorful cats (page 27): thin card stock, pencil, scissors, thick white paper, paper clips, bright paints, sponge, colored card stock, glue, strip of card stock

Rainy racehorse (page 29): pencil, blue pastel paper, soft pastels or chalks

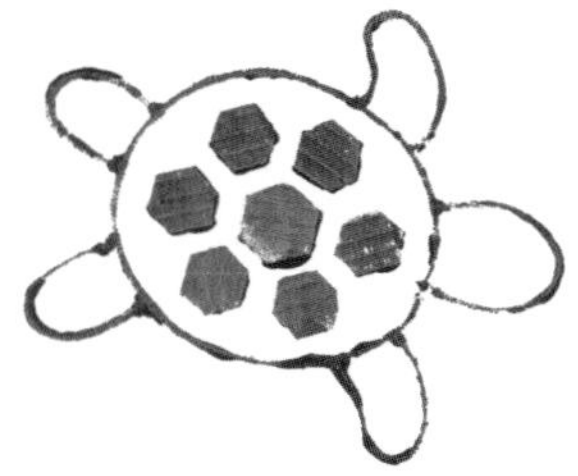

INDEX